24/7 DHARMA

2 4 / 7 D H A R M A

IMPERMANENCE, NO-SELF, NIRVANA

Dennis Genpo Merzel

Journey Editions

Boston · Tokyo · Singapore

First published in 2001 by Journey Editions, an imprint of Periplus Editions (HK) Ltd., with editorial offices at 153 Milk Street, Boston, Massachusetts, 02109.

Library of Congress Cataloging-in-Publication Data in Process

Merzel, Dennis Genpo, 1944-
   24/7 Dharma : impermanence, no-self, nirvana / Dennis Merzel.
   p. cm.
  ISBN 1-58290-047-7
  1. Buddhism--Doctrines. 2. Spiritual life--Buddhism. I. Title.
BQ4260 .M47 2001
294.3'4--dc21

00-058969

Distributed by

North America	Japan	Asia Pacific
Tuttle Publishing	Tuttle Publishing	Berkeley Books Pte Ltd
Distribution Center	RK Building, 2nd Floor	5 Little Road #08-01
Airport Industrial Park	2-13-10 Shimo-Meguro, Meguro-Ku	Singapore 536983
364 Innovation Drive	Tokyo 153 0064	Tel: (65) 280-1330
North Clarendon, VT 05759-9436	Tel: (03) 5437-0171	Fax: (65) 280-6290
Tel: (802) 773-8930	Tel: (03) 5437-0755	
Tel: (800) 526-2778		
Fax: (802) 773-6993		

06 05 04 03 02 01   9 8 7 6 5 4 3 2 1

Printed in the United States of America

To my wife, Stephanie Young Merzel

and my children, Tai and Nicole

CONTENTS

A LETTER FROM THE AUTHOR

Twenty-five hundred years ago, Shakyamuni Buddha declared that all beings are enlightened; they have the same wisdom, the same virtue, the same compassion as the Buddha.

Zen in its essence is pure, genuine, free from beliefs and dogmas. The moment all seeking has ceased and all searching has come to an end, then one experiences the freedom and joy of just being truly oneself, complete and whole. Zen is in the very experiencing of this truth of life, in the awakening to our true self and to the love and compassion that comes from this realization.

This Dharma can be lost in our generation if you don't manifest it. There is only one in the universe, and that one is you. If you don't practice, it won't be realized. If you don't realize it, it won't be accomplished. When you die, the world dies. You are the world.

—Dennis Genpo Merzel

EDITOR'S
PREFACE

Why do we suffer? How can we free ourselves from fear and stress? What is our true nature? What does it take to live in harmony with ourselves and with each other?

In this book Genpo Roshi addresses these ultimate questions. Bringing to life the universal truths Buddha taught twenty-five centuries ago, he evokes the immediate experience of Zen for the reader of today. *24/7 Dharma* clarifies what is true for all of us at all times—twenty-four hours a day, seven days a week—whatever our religious or cultural background.

Shakyamuni Buddha gave his life completely to the crucial problem of human suffering. All he cared about was that we liberate ourselves from bondage to fear and pain and live our lives in freedom.

The structure of this book is based upon the Three Dharma Seals, three truths that are essential to Buddha's teaching. As Genpo Roshi presents them, the first is *Impermanence:* We and our whole reality are in a state of flux and constant change. The second is *No-self:* No one has any fixed or permanent self. The third is *Nirvana:* When we recognize our true nature, this very life is the liberation from suffering.

The Three Dharma Seals are principles of direct experience, not articles of blind belief, and can be realized and manifested by anyone who takes time enough to study this life, sitting quietly in meditation. When we acknowledge our impermanence and the ever-changing nature of all things, we are immediately intimate with the suffering of all who feel afflicted by change, and we know the cause of that suffering. Finding no fixed self separate from others, we naturally experience compassion for all beings. We want others to awaken to their true nature and appreciate their lives in freedom.

In the twenty-five hundred years since Buddha's teaching was first expounded, this Dharma has been practiced in many countries and passed down to us through a variety of cultures. Here today a living American Zen Master clarifies these ancient truths in a dynamic contemporary voice.

This book consists of selected excerpts from Genpo Roshi's teachings over the past two decades. You can open anywhere to find something that appeals to you, or you can read the book from beginning to end as a continuous evocation of truth—day by day, moment by moment, living your life, being your true self.

—*Stephen Muho Proskauer*

ACKNOWLEDGMENTS

The influence of my wife Stephanie inspired a shift in my perspective over the past five years, which is responsible for much of the teaching in this book. Three of my students deserve credit for the conception and creation of 24/7 *Dharma*. Tenkei Coppens Sensei originally proposed the idea of publishing a collection of brief quotations extracted from my talks over many years. The production of the book then involved countless hours of work by Wynn Wright, who reviewed and transcribed most of the talks from which the recent excerpts were taken, and chose some of the quotations, and by Stephen Proskauer, who selected, edited, and arranged excerpts from twenty years of teaching to create these chapters.

We are indebted to Jan Johnson and Michael Kerber at Journey Editions for their invaluable assistance in refining the focus and organization of the book. Kanzeon students and friends too numerous to name assisted with transcription and editorial review, including especially Meg Meiser and

George Robertson. In fact, everyone at Kanzeon Zen Center contributed directly or indirectly to this project whether they realize it or not, and I want to take this opportunity to express my heartfelt thanks to all these students for their sincere efforts to manifest and share the Dharma.

Finally, I offer this little book in deepest gratitude to Taizan Maezumi Roshi, my esteemed teacher for twenty-four years, who passed away five years ago. I hope it will further his lifelong mission of spreading the Dharma in the West.

—Dennis Genpo Merzel
Salt Lake City
May 2000

SUFFERING

A ll of Zen, all of Buddhism, is about the same thing: your life—your own suffering and how to go beyond this suffering.

Once we become open and vulnerable, we see suffering wherever we turn. That's what happened to Shakyamuni Buddha. After twenty-nine years cooped up in the unreal world of the palace, enjoying himself with beautiful young people, Buddha escaped with his charioteer.

Imagine his shock when he saw the real world for the first time: people stooped and shriveled with age, sick and dying on the street; corpses lying in the gutter! Think how vulnerable he must have felt after leading such a protected life.

From that point on, his only concern was to understand the cause of suffering and find the way to put an end to it.

B uddha used the word *duhkha*, which is usually translated as *unsatisfactoriness* or *suffering*, but literally refers to a stuck axle that won't turn. When we are stuck, not willing to flow with life's changes, we suffer.

S uffering results from attachment and aversion. There are four basic reasons why we suffer: wanting what we don't have or resenting what we have; longing for a loved one who isn't there or despising the person who is with us.

W e are deluded. We think there is something to find. Seeking for something only leads to suffering. So to put an end to suffering, all we have to do is to stop seeking, craving, and wanting.

Knowing this simple truth, we distract ourselves continuously in countless ways, resisting, ignoring what is right in front of us. Our deepest yearning to be liberated, to be at peace, goes unsatisfied. We continue grasping, and the wheel of life and death, the wheel of suffering, turns on and on and on.

How do we put an end to this delusion, this ignorance, this suffering? How do we cease wanting, when almost every living moment we exist in a state of craving?

Shakyamuni Buddha discovered a way to do that, called *dhyana* in his day, later *ch'an* in China and *zazen* in Japan—to sit still with one's spine erect and naturally relaxed and just be, not doing anything.

Sitting in zazen, Buddha identified the cause of suffering as ignorance or wrong understanding, an upside-down view of reality. This view is based on dualistic thinking: good/bad, mine/yours, self/other, inside/outside. Our discriminating mind gives rise to desire and craving, attachment and aversion, hate and fear. Liberation from suffering means going beyond dualistic thinking.

As long as there is still wanting and craving, there is still attachment to an ego self. This self *is* suffering! When we are holding onto the self, this body and mind, we will suffer.

Why? Attachment causes suffering and we are dependent on everything to survive. There are so many things—such as air, water, and food—that we depend on. Without these things there would be no life, so we are completely dependent and attached, and we suffer.

T here is a huge difference between pain and suffering. As long as we have a physical body, there will be pain. It's just the nature of the game.

But then we add something extra that we call "suffering" on top of our pain. Buddha taught how to free oneself from this suffering—how to live with pain, not how to get rid of pain.

When there is pain, be pain! When there's joy, be joy! The secret is not to create a separation from the pain, trying to get rid of it, but actually to be it completely.

A s an athlete I never really minded pain; I saw it as something to conquer, because I was choosing it. If I stopped competing, the pain would stop. When you are choosing the pain and the challenge of going beyond pain, it can even be exhilarating.

But when we are subject to pain that we are not choosing, it is a very different experience. That's real pain! We can't make it stop, and this teaches us a whole different lesson about life. It allows us to appreciate the pain that others are going through.

The more we get in touch with our own vulnerability and mortality, the more we come to appreciate our life and the preciousness of each moment. Life is the real teacher. The beginning of accomplishment in Zen is realizing the preciousness of life.

How can we appreciate life without appreciating suffering? Unless we know intimately what suffering is, how can we really appreciate another's suffering?

It would be like trying to appreciate a fine melon without ever having tasted one. You might think you could appreciate it, but could you really?

S uffering has to be our own genuine experience. When we own our suffering we know directly, intimately, what Buddha was talking about when he said, "You are born, you grow old, you get sick, you die."

This may not be a pleasant picture, but if we can really accept it, right there is the freedom: We are facing reality, not escaping into some illusion.

How could we really know what we have unless we have experienced losing it? While we have it we don't appreciate it. Only after we lose it do we really value what we had.

L ife is very fragile, very precious. Realizing this, we have more willingness to face whatever gift life brings us. The experience of doing that over and over again gives us faith and courage to keep going.

Taking life as it comes, not knowing what will happen next, we can be fully present each moment to experience whatever it is. If it is suffering, we suffer; if it is pleasure, we have pleasure.

IMPERMANENCE

All form is constantly in flux, constantly changing—even stones, rocks. We don't see it normally, but even so the rock is changing, being worn away. The earth, the sun, the moon, everything; all form is changing. We call this change emptiness, because it's not fixed. It's not really solid in the sense of permanent. It's impermanent, therefore changing, therefore empty.

The first time you sit down and look within, what do you see? The mind is chaotic, in constant flux. Everything is continually changing. There isn't anything you can really hold onto. All things simply arise and cease. All phenomena are truly empty, and this very body and mind is also empty.

There's a certain flexibility of mind that arises as we sit and we see constant movement and change. We start to see that the mind wants to become fixated on something, wants to hold on. But we can't hold on, so we begin to just relax and let go. This creates a certain fluidity and flexibility that can be communicated by just being what you are.

W hen you're just sitting, your mind is truly open, not trying to do anything. You're sitting there doing nothing, watching the rising and falling of all phenomena—of thoughts, of sensations, of feelings. You're not trying to exclude or reject anything and you're not holding onto anything that comes up.

When you sit like that, it's called choiceless awareness or unsurpassable awareness. You're simply being that big, open, empty space that allows whatever appears to appear and whatever goes to go.

W hen we sit and do nothing, we knock the stuffing out of something; we knock the substantiality out of it. When we sit and do nothing, everything that seems so substantial, solid, stuffed, is now seen as empty. Not empty in the sense of an empty cup, but empty in the sense of insubstantial, that the very form itself is formless.

Not only is the cup empty, the material the cup is made of is also empty. This very form, this very body, is insubstantial. This very full container is already empty. So if you're already empty, what is there to do?

If everything were solid and permanent and fixed, then there would be no life. Everything would be static and dead. There would be no life because there would be no possibility for change.

T he mind that creates no walls, no barriers, that has no abiding place, no footholds, is a beginner's mind. It is one with the continuous movement of life. Completely, fully, endlessly moving on. Exploring, realizing, experiencing whatever comes up. Only a mind like this can be truly joyful, always fresh and new.

The mind includes everything. Nothing separate exists. There is just now, just this moment, with everything changing constantly. When we are really abiding in the moment, it is changing too fast to hold onto, too fast to analyze or judge or label.

It's like a flowing river. The river flows very fast, very deep and wide. Constant movement, constant flow. This flowing river is life, is reality. But because the movement is so swift, because it is constantly changing and impermanent, we seek something permanent. We seek something safe and secure.

It is as though we were to get out of the river and dig a hole on the riverbank. The hole fills up with water. Looking for something safe and secure, something we can depend on, we play in that little pool beside the river.

What we are missing is being one with the flowing river, with life itself, with reality. It takes tremendous courage and faith to climb out of the little pool that has become dead, stagnant, and lifeless and jump back into the flowing river of life.

What happens when you are just sitting in the mountains alongside a river or stream? You can hear the sounds of moving water, the current hitting against the banks and stones. It's always moving, going deeper, wider, with no beginning and no end, just continuously flowing.

In the stagnant pool movement is constrained. There is no flow. And yet this is what we seek for and create in our lives.

In order to keep our personal or societal existence safe and predictable, we will fight and even kill, all because we are looking for a sense of permanence. But life is not permanent or fixed. This is one of Buddha's central teachings.

Hold onto no position. Be unfixed. Then you perceive everything in a totally different light and your unlimited mind is functioning perfectly.

U sually we're fighting the flow, trying to swim upstream, wanting something we can't have, having something we don't want, always struggling. It's this kind of desiring and seeking that keeps us from really being free.

Instead, realize what your karma is and stop fighting it. Follow the flow of the stream. As soon as we turn around and go with it, it's no longer painful. The resistance is what creates the struggle. It's just like two hands that are constantly struggling against each other. As soon as one hand stops resisting, the other hand can go free.

Our relationships are the same way. All a person has to do is give up trying to be right; step aside, be empty, be selfless—or at least try to approach that state. As soon as the resistance is gone, both persons are free to grow and mature. Instead, we're constantly struggling, hanging onto our own positions and ideas, preventing not only ourselves from growing, but others as well.

W e are always searching for a state of permanence. We want good things and wonderful feelings to last forever and that which is painful or uncomfortable to end as quickly as possible.

We fear change and so we create beliefs, religious institutions, philosophies, political theories, and economic systems that reinforce the illusion of security and safety. We are afraid we will lose what we have attained—our families, jobs, homes, positions, possessions, knowledge, and accomplishments.

Our fear of change and our greed to control have caused us to become attached to what we have and how we live. We have slowly been stopping the flow of the river from bringing fresh new water to revitalize our stagnant pool. Little by little we have been deadening our experience of life.

Our mind cannot accept the fact that life, like a river, is forever moving on, flowing and changing. The mind fears death. It fears living in an impermanent, insecure world. So it builds walls around itself to protect its very existence, the walls of *me* and *mine, my* beliefs and ideas.

These walls limit our experience of life, of reality. They give us the illusion of protection, yet they cause us to live in confusion, fear, and misery, isolated and struggling to maintain our little world. Life is flowing on endlessly, constantly changing and attempting to break down these artificial walls we have made.

When we always seek permanence and security while resisting pain, discomfort, and fear, we can be enticed into a life of greed, corruption, and evil in order to maintain our comfort. Once caught in such a position, we are afraid to come out, to explore, to understand our own mind, to live life fully, to encounter truth, reality, God.

When we experience life fully, one with the flow of life, not rejecting or protecting our self, we bring love to whatever it is we do. There is not the element of doing or giving for some personal gain afterwards. It is more like a child who does what he does with just the pure love of doing.

When we do things simply because we love to do them, not out of shoulds and should-nots, we need no gimmicks, no techniques. Life is fully lived and experienced in each moment with complete awareness and consciousness. It is like a good bonfire that burns itself out completely, leaving no trace behind.

NO-SELF

YOU ARE NOT WHAT YOU THINK

We are always trying to do something or become something or be somebody. And in this having to be somebody we create all our problems, all our difficulties, because right there the ego comes popping up. If somebody disagrees with our understanding or our opinion, we're upset, because our ideas and concepts are what make up this so-called self.

When we let go of everything coming and going, when we really see into the flux, the nature that's constantly changing, we cease being attached to our egoistic views. We see that our natural state is already empty. We have clouded it over, covered it with this concept of self.

We believe this body is the extent of our life. We identify with this body as who we are, and we see everything else as being separate and apart from our self. We see others as external things. We see the sun, the moon, the mountains, rivers, oceans, trees, the flowers, and the grasses, all as separate from our self.

And because this particular belief is so strong, because it's such a strong conditioning, we're not even aware of it as a belief. We just take it as the truth, as a fact. This false belief is what keeps us bound, imprisoned. It keeps us so self-conscious that we're always watching, always judging, always evaluating our self.

Because of our belief in being separate, we fall into all kinds of harmful actions and deeds that create more problems for us. Competitiveness is a big one—trying to get ahead of others, stepping on each other. We become frustrated and angry with each other. We try to control others and we condemn them. All of these things stem from one false belief, "I am apart, separate from everything else."

After we are born and have lived some years, we create a false separation between our self and others, beginning with mother and then with other people and the environment. We begin to identify our self as a separate individual.

As soon as we do that, we enclose and limit our self. We think of our self as residing in this body, maybe in the head. We identify with this body or with our mind as who we are and create a false barrier or membrane, an invisible membrane that separates us from everything else—from earth, from sky, from other beings, human and non-human. As soon as we do that, we create this inner "me" and that outer "not-me." A lot of problems arise from this division, because anything considered not me or outside of the membrane poses the potential threat of destroying the "me."

It's like a bubble on the surface of the ocean. Anything that might puncture the very thin membrane that allows me to be a separate individual is a threat and is regarded with skepticism, paranoia, fear. The important thing becomes maintaining this identity to be sure that "me" continues to exist in the form I've become familiar with, the known.

Allowing the membrane to break would be merging into the unknown, a state of just being, returning to original nature, which is expanded consciousness. All the past and all the future, all space and all time, are included right now, right here. The ego fears this merging more than anything else in the world, because in that state the "me" disappears.

When there's me-ness or ego, everything revolves around "me" and there is a tremendous self-centeredness or self-concern. We see our self and our life as extremely important. We see everything we do as the center of the universe, and all our problems are magnified.

The way to go beyond viewing the world from this narrow perspective is to expand consciousness, expand the mind, so there is no outside, no outer boundary, no membrane. Then there's neither outside nor inside and everything is included.

What that takes is becoming very quiet, very still and quiet, and allowing the mind to expand in all directions simultaneously and infinitely. Nothing is excluded and you see everything as yourself. You're not separated from it. Then the state of merging can happen all the time.

When there is fear, you know you are once again creating a barrier between yourself and the world, between yourself and others.

I f we look carefully, we see that all suffering and dissatisfaction seem to come down to one basic point. Because of the notion that we are a separate entity, somehow we are never happy and satisfied with the way things are.

We hold certain opinions according to our different training and experience as scientist, artist, therapist, teacher, or whatever occupation we may hold. We don't see the same reality as others. We sift everything through this view that we hold on life, and we don't even realize that's what we're doing. We get locked into a fixed position, an egoistic view.

Then it's not two human beings relating to one another; it's two views relating to each other. We don't even have a relationship with our husband or wife or children or parents. There are just two views on life trying to relate. That's why we have such hard times with each other. We can't seem to be in harmony and get along because we have different views that we take for reality. We think others should have the same view, but it's impossible. They can't. We have our karma; they have theirs.

W e are conditioned beings with patterns and habits that cause us and those around us a lot of grief, pain, confusion, anger, hatred, jealousy, envy, pettiness—all kinds of suffering. Maybe the basic reason we keep falling back into these habitual patterns is self-centeredness. When we see our self as the center and separate from everyone and everything else, we have to continuously protect and guard this self.

If we think back over how we learned what we now know as our life and our perspective on life, we see that it's all taught. In fact, there have probably been few moments when we had an original idea. It's all conditioned! At some point, we see our conditioning and we want to be free. We want to liberate ourselves because we see, "I'm not my conditioning! That's not who I am."

SO JUST LET IT GO

We're taught to have all kinds of preferences and dislikes for everything. Sitting there, we begin to see how we've got something to say about everything that comes up.

The only way we can be free is to let go of these likes and dislikes. But when we do that, it feels like we're going to lose our life, because that's all our identity has been—our views, concepts, and notions.

B uddha said that the cause of our stress and pain is that we don't have a proper perspective. Somehow we see things in an upside-down way.

What is this wrong perspective? My one perspective! We don't think of it as just one perspective; we think of it as the *only* perspective.

How does this translate into our daily lives? Don't we often see others as wrong because they don't share our perspective? This causes constant clashes in relationships. The ego gets involved and we can't find our way out.

We become blind to everything but our own view. We can't see it's just one view. Why get so tied up with it?

E ach perspective is not only right but simultaneously wrong, because every perspective is just a piece of the pie, not the whole thing.

How strong our addiction is to wanting to be right! We really cling to being right, and it's amazing the cost. It costs us nothing less than our complete life—our freedom, happiness, and peace. Yet we would rather continue to suffer, to be on whatever ego trip we're on, to feel fragmented and disenchanted—along with all the ramifications of loneliness, fear, anxiety, depression, and anger that are always right there—than just admit we are wrong.

B ecause we see our self as a separate entity apart from everything else, we fear that we will be crushed or destroyed. Someone out there can kill me or make me look bad, or I won't be able to cope with the situation, or I am going to look stupid.

We have regrets about the past and fear about the future. What is past? It doesn't exist. The past is memory. What about the future? Does it exist? No, it is just concepts and projections. There is only now.

Does now exist? Close your eyes and look into your own mind and see what is between the thoughts. Is there any content in that "now"? What exists there between the thoughts? Anything? Or just space?

They say that the truth will set you free. But the price of admission is one life. In a way, this practice is a kind of suicide. The ego ends up destroying itself.

E very time our world seems to be cracking like a piece of glass, we start putting it all back together, when in fact our glass house has to shatter.

There is tremendous fear of ceasing to exist as you know yourself. It would seem like dying. Something has to become more important than your fear of death.

The ego wants to be awake and witness its own destruction. It wants to be there, so we make it right to be aware. When we make anything right, everything other than that becomes wrong. Now we are stuck again, thinking that being conscious and aware is better than being unconscious and unaware.

But if we stop picking and choosing, we find that sometimes we're awake and sometimes we're not. Whatever is, is. When you are beyond caring whether you're awake or not awake, you're free.

We have so many ideas, and we are so attached to them! We would probably rather die, go through hell, or kill someone than really let go of our attachment to ideas. Thinking we know, thinking we're right, we just do not want to relinquish our position.

Now why would that be, if letting go is the only thing standing between you and truly manifesting your true potential as a human being, to be awake and conscious, fully present? The answer is *fear*.

W hen you have the willingness to face your fear, fear is nothing, just another big concept—maybe overwhelming, but basically just an idea. You have to be willing to face your fear and go through your doubt and let it all go.

I f I were to sum up the whole practice of Zen in one word, it would be *relinquishment*. It comes down to complete relinquishment, moment by moment. What we are learning is to keep letting go, and it takes a tremendous amount of trust and courage.

T o truly give is to give up the self. To let go of the self, to relinquish the self, that's true giving.

W hen you relinquish, then you expand. When you drop the identification with your body and mind, when you let go, you expand beyond yourself, you experience ecstasy and bliss.

You can't experience the ecstasy or the bliss and hold onto your body and mind, onto yourself. It never works. That's the ego trying to experience ecstasy. The ego has to die, let go; then you experience ecstasy, not before.

Tremendous fear comes up when we begin to let go of our concepts of who we are. In this practice we come to realize everything is okay as it is, even if you know you are going to die soon. You get to a view where you see everything is happening perfectly. So if you are losing your grip on who you thought you were, just trust that it's okay.

You may lose one concept or picture of yourself, but you'll form a new one. Then you work on letting the new one go, because you discovered how liberating it is to have no picture. After that happens over and over, you begin to see that something does go on.

At some point you finally realize that your picture of yourself is all concepts, just ideas and notions. We have created a bunch of ideas and put them together to make a picture. It's very liberating to lose the picture and to come back to not knowing.

When you have faith in something, it's not faith, it's belief. When you have faith in nothing, what is this no-thing? Emptiness, true nature. Your true nature is no-nature. Having faith in no-thing is trusting in your true nature.

One way you can see faith is in relationship to your willingness to let go of preconceived ideas and notions. The tighter you hold on, the less faith you have. The more open and willing you are to let go, the more faith you have.

A quiet mind looks like death to the little mind, the ego. It looks like death or madness, because we are so used to a busy, active mind. When the mind quiets down and there's space, we think that we're going out of our mind, which in fact is true. We go into our body, into the *hara* (the lower belly), and out of the head, where we usually reside.

At that moment, not only is our sitting very solid and stable, like a mountain or a boulder, but our life becomes much more centered and stable—not fixed on our ideas or opinions—fluid and flexible, yet strong, like the strength of a tree that can bend.

EXPERIENCE NO-SELF

B reathing is always present, always here. It's always with you. If you
stop breathing, you're not living anymore. As long as you're alive,
you're breathing, in and out. And when you really become breathing itself,
or what we term "being one with the breath," there is just breathing.
There's no distinction, no separation, between the inside and the outside,
the external and internal, between oneself and everything else. So we
make an effort to sit on the cushion, quiet the mind, and be aware of the
breath—to be just breathing.

When we really become breathing itself or sitting itself, even the
effort drops away. It becomes effortless—just sitting, just breathing—
because there's no one making the effort. There is no one breathing.
There's no one even being breathed. Breathing is breathing. Zazen is
doing zazen. Just sitting.

When you follow the breath, other things will come up, especially sensations in the body, such as pain. When you have body sensations, it's okay to notice them and place your attention on them. Feelings will tend to disperse or disappear with awareness.

It's as if the awareness were a beam of light. When you bring the light of attention to a sensation, that sensation will gradually dissolve by itself. So if there's tension in your body, bring your awareness to that place of tension. Stay relaxed. Relax right into it. Don't avoid or resist it. And by just bringing your awareness or attention to that area, the tension will disappear.

The more we tense up with pain, the worse it becomes. The more we relax with the pain, the more quickly it just disappears by itself. Make pain your friend, your intimate friend, because pain allows you to be present, right here and now.

Don't try to run away from it. That's what our life tends to be about—the avoidance of pain, the avoidance of fear. We become the victim—the victim of our life, the victim of our self, the victim of everything.

When you start sitting, what do you see about your mind? It is just utter chaos. Now do you wonder why you wouldn't look before?

With practice we can discover moments of sanity in all of this chaos. But we have to learn to see the thoughts for what they are, just thoughts; the feelings for what they are, just feelings; and the emotions for what they are, just emotions.

It doesn't mean we stop feeling these emotions. As we practice longer, maybe we can feel the feelings even more deeply. We can be more sensitive, more vulnerable, because we can have another perspective at the same time—that, really, it's not the end of the world. So my ego was destroyed again. My pride was destroyed again. I lost it again. Our practice is one of letting go of attachment to the notion of self.

W hen you truly trust yourself, you can drop the self, you can let go of body and mind. If you can't trust yourself enough to give up yourself, how can you trust someone else? Our whole practice comes down to this point: faith and trust in yourself, which is no-self.

We can even see something very positive every time we experience something very negative. Each time we go through some horrible experience, what do we find at the end? A new insight, a new awareness, a new perspective, a new self. A new self, again and again.

Our true nature is as fluid as water. So when we really begin to see the emptiness of all phenomena, the emptiness of self, when we're really intimate with our true nature, we become unfixed, as fluid as water.

L ook into your own mind, the source from which thoughts arise. What hears the sounds? Look and you find only empty nothing. And yet, something's hearing, something's seeing, something's experiencing pain. What is it? It can't be anything but yourself, your true self.

But somehow we can't accept this. We continually go on looking and seeking. Only convince yourself to stop seeking. Once and for all, convince yourself there is nothing to seek, nothing to attain, and then just sit, nothing left to do, nothing left to search for.

There are some meditation practices where the goal is to become the witness. There is nothing wrong with that; but if you only get to the point of witnessing, you never come to realize that there is no witness.

When you practice just sitting, you start at this point. You're already there. By practicing non-doing, you're already bridging the gap. You're doing something to do nothing.

How do you carry this into your daily life? When you do something completely, when you give yourself completely to it, there's no you, there's no self, there is just the doing.

E veryone is the Buddha. Everything is the Buddha. But if you search for Buddha you can't find Buddha. You'll just find grass and trees, birds and flowers, blue sky and white clouds. This formless form that's listening to the birds, that is the mind of the Buddha. That is your body.

Whatever you perceive, you are. When you perceive a bird, you are that bird. When you perceive a flower, you are that flower. When Shakyamuni Buddha held up a flower, the whole universe was that flower.

ADMIT YOU ARE BUDDHA

To realize that you are the living Buddha, the awakened one, is probably the most incredible experience you could ever have in your entire life. It could blow your mind.

Y ou realize from beginningless beginning you have been complete and whole as you are. And this supreme truth is the most difficult for us to swallow. There's nothing to be attained.

First we look for the Buddha outside our self, as some perfect being. It's so easy to hold an image of perfection in our head and place this image on a deceased person who can no longer speak and disillusion us. Then we strive to become perfect like that person.

What's wrong with striving to become perfect? The striving itself, since we are already perfect just as we are. The desire to become something other than what we are arises from dualistic thinking and creates suffering.

There is no Buddha outside yourself. There is no Dharma outside yourself. There is no practice outside yourself and there is no Way apart from yourself. You are the living Buddha. You are the breathing Dharma. You are the practice. You are the Way. We each have to get to the place where at least we can admit to that.

S ince we are all Buddha to begin with, why do we need to practice and realize it? Because there is a world of difference between understanding this on an intellectual, conceptual level and really appreciating it on the deepest level of your being. One keeps you in bondage, the other sets you free.

The great masters all say the same thing: From the very beginning, innately we are completely awakened, completely enlightened, free, unhindered. It is only due to our dualistic way of thinking that we believe that somehow we're not.

Our little mind always wants to arrive at a conclusion, to reach a finish line. It cannot fathom infinity, eternity. This mind thinks in terms of beginning and end. When we can fathom infinity, we're not using our mind. It's only when the mind lets go of itself that we can experience infinity, the Unborn, God, Buddha.

Your own mind is as vast and wide and boundless as the whole cosmos. Ideas, concepts are puny little things. Do you have more faith in them than you do in the teachings of the Buddha and the great masters? Do you put more trust in ideas and beliefs than in your own true self?

The true self is not limited to this world or even to this universe. It has no boundaries, no fixed position, no form, no self, no limits, no time. It's totally beyond knowing or not knowing, being or not being—totally beyond all discrimination. That's what we have to realize. This formless form is none other than this very form, this very body, this very life!

DWELL IN THE UNBORN MIND

M ind is ungraspable. It's also empty. When we look, we see this very
mind is no-mind. It has no boundary, no outside, no limit. This
mind is universal mind, what we call the Unborn Buddha Mind. This
Unborn Mind is manifesting in each one of us.

W hat is it worth to live in the Unborn Mind perspective, to make that shift and let go moment by moment by moment by moment, to really live the now?

The cost is your life. And if you have any picture in your mind of what it's supposed to look like, that's just an obstacle.

We want the explosion before we give up the self. We want the experience while the self is intact. We want to hold onto our self, to our experiencer, and have that Great Experience. But the Great Experience is when we have dropped the experiencer. This is the experience of no-experience and the preaching that has never been preached. This is the Dharma that has never been taught. This is No-Buddha and No-Dharma. What is it? It can't be expressed. And yet, it's being expressed constantly.

With our limited mind we see our self as a tiny being at the center of the universe and the whole world as out there separate from us. It is simply impossible for this small mind to wrap itself around the Unborn Mind. How can a small, limited mind grasp the unlimited? Whatever your little mind grasps is no longer the unlimited, ungraspable Unborn Buddha Mind.

The moment the little mind gives up trying to grasp the infinite, trying to reach egohood and be the almighty one, at that very moment there is vast openness and the Unborn Buddha Mind is present.

T he barriers that separate you from me, outside from inside, will dissolve. The mind will be open, aware, alert—not burdened with its own accumulations, acquisitions, ideologies, beliefs, knowledge, and old experiences. This expanded mind, which is boundless, lives timelessly, spaciously, without concern for security.

To such a mind, life is truly extraordinary. A mind such as this is one with life itself, one with the Dharma. This is what we call the Buddha Mind, because it is awakened to the reality of life, moment to moment. It is an all-inclusive mind, nothing excluded from it.

M ost of us live with the idea that we know who we are. But really, who we are is so big that we can't get our mind around it. We can't conceive of it because it is unlimited. We can't grasp who we are and so we can never really know.

So you are closer to the truth when you don't know who you are, and that's very liberating.

You have to realize that true nature is no-nature, no-mind, unborn and undying. This Buddha Mind is what you have innately. You are born with the Unborn Buddha Mind.

O ne of our false beliefs is that our true nature, our Buddha nature, somehow exists apart from our very body and mind, bigger than it and yet including it. Another false belief commonly held is that this body and mind is the true self, that there is no self beyond this body and mind. A third false notion is that somewhere within this body exists a true self.

Now, what notion is left? If you hold any concept of it, it's false. Can you live without holding any notion, any idea of what it is?

Maybe we should change the question. Can you really live while continuing to hold onto any notion or concept of what *it* is? As long as you have a notion of *it*, that is not *it* and you cannot live freely, truly.

There's a big difference between thinking you know or believing you know or having faith that you know and really knowing, the kind of knowing that's beyond knowing and not knowing.

We have to remember our true nature. We have to begin the search all over again until we remember through direct experience.

O ur true mind doesn't need to be anybody or anything special, because it is everything, all things. It is already innately one with all phenomena. From the beginning nothing in our true nature is lacking. Nothing is missing. So why should it need to become something?

Why shouldn't I be special? The answer is very simple: You already are. You don't need to become special or prove that you're special. Everyone is already the living Buddha, complete, whole, perfect as you are. All this action and effort to become special is just making you very unspecial and creating a tremendous amount of pain and suffering.

W hat are we here for? To have direct experience of our true nature, the Unborn Buddha Mind. Because it is unnameable, it has many names. But, it has no characteristics, no form, no shape, no color, no size.

What greater gift could you have been born with than this? Why continually trade it in for a mind that is self-centered, always trying to be right, arguing, getting angry, feeling deficient and needy. Would you really rather be a fighting spirit or a hungry ghost?

Why not just dwell in the Unborn from this moment forth? Master Bankei used to say that if you abide in it for just thirty days, you will always dwell in it.

This very mind is unborn and undying. Ungraspable. Unattainable. Inconceivable. When you look for it, you can't find it. And yet you're using it all the time. You're never lacking it.

When we meditate, we return to fundamental sanity, reality, our natural state of being. The pure and natural state is just to be. Everything comes out of that.

Sometime in your life you may have experienced this fundamental reality. It could have been in the mountains or listening to music. In some way you have tasted pure being, the stillness where everything is perfect as it is. In this moment nothing is left out, nothing is in excess. This moment is timeless. Sitting meditation seems to be the most direct route to this experience.

When we sit we are coming home to our most natural state of being. We are returning to ordinary mind. The trip we've taken for most of our lives has drawn us further and further away from this natural state of being.

The first time we sit down we already have the sense of coming home. Over time, this feeling grows more and more, and we find that home is not some place out there, but wherever we are.

W hat could be closer to our natural functioning than just being? Everything else is something added on top of that. The purest state of mind is sitting and just being.

It is very difficult to just let things be. It is too difficult to control ourselves, so we try to control the people close to us, such as our kids, spouse, or parents. We even try to control the environment.

In zazen, you learn to allow everything to be as it is. You just sit there and allow everything to do its thing. You discover it all happens very nicely without your help. The rain comes, the rain stops. Birds chirp, they stop chirping. The traffic comes, it quiets down. Everything just goes on very well without your help. What a relief—you're not that important!

So just tell yourself, "Let it be," and allow things to be as they are. It starts with sitting and then carries over into the rest of your life. Things seem to get easier and easier as we stop trying to control everyone and everything.

When you get past all the chaos and clutter in your mind, you experience the now, the present. When you experience this present, you experience infinity. The mind can never grasp infinity. It's always beyond the reach of the mind, because the mind as we know it is too limited. We have to go beyond the mind.

From the ego or small mind point of view, we see practice and realization as a gradual step-by-step process taking a long time. We have some insight, then we fall back into confusion. Later we have another insight; it clouds over and we are back into confusion again. From the ego's perspective, this is how Zen practice goes; it takes time.

From the point of view of our true nature, it's not a matter of time, it's not a matter of practice or training or even realization. There is nothing to be realized, nothing to be practiced, nothing to be attained.

What's lacking? When you are one with the Unborn Mind, what can be missing? What can be extra, in excess? And how could it be a matter of time? It's far beyond time. It's the eternal now, the timeless, the ever-present.

What happens if you realize that your mind is unlimited, boundless, and has always been from the beginningless beginning to the endless end? Your priorities about everything change immediately.

You stop operating out of fear of losing—losing control, losing concepts, losing identity, losing things, losing your mind. What do you call that when you stop fearing loss? Liberation!

You stand alone on the sublime peak. You were born alone, you live alone, and you die alone. Above the heavens and below the heavens you are the only one, the Holy One, the Supreme One. Just simply, you forgot.

T aking a leap into the unknown is called a glimpse, an opening. Doing this continuously, moment to moment, is embodying or manifesting it.

Having an opening is *seeing* it; Great Enlightenment is *being* it.

If you attach to any experience, even that of enlightenment—everything perfect as is—then it becomes just another fantasy you hold onto.

During the time when you abide in that experience, as Buddha did for forty-nine days, things are tremendously radiant. There's tremendous love and light and energy; but even this has to be relinquished. Eventually you have to drop it, let it go, and become completely ordinary.

We're practicing Zen to go from this shore, the world of bondage and suffering, to the other shore, the realm of liberation and bliss. But this is a big delusion! I can hardly say it with a straight face, because there aren't two separate shores.

When you reach the other shore, you find out the two shores are identical, only now *you* have gone. Liberation and suffering—they're identical. Freedom and imprisonment—identical. All the opposites are identical. There's no place to go; you have already gone beyond.

This is it! Paradise is not in the future, it's not going to come. As my son, Tai, would say, "It doesn't get any better than this."

C ast away anything you think you have attained, anything you think you've realized, because in the end the truth is that there is nothing to be realized.

When Dogen Zenji returned from China after six years studying with Tendo Nyojo, dropping off body and mind, the first thing he said was, "I return empty-handed, not even a speck of Dharma do I have. The sun rises in the east, sets in the west. My eyes are horizontal, my nose is vertical. That's what I realized."

To live without goals, without ambition, brings up fear. We fear we are not going to be motivated, we are not going to get anywhere, we are not going to get results.

Nothing further to do, no place to go—then what? What are we going to do with our life? We're so used to seeking, we're scared to death of not having anything further to seek after, of being nothing. We're so frightened we just hold on with all our might to the idea that there's something to seek, something to attain, something to realize.

T rying to become anything is wasting your time. When you're busy doing something, seeking something, going after something, you're not living in the present.

Doing nothing is not wasting your time. It is the only thing that's not wasting your time, because when you are doing nothing you are totally present. You are living fully, here and now in this present moment, alert and awake.

O ur practice is like a spiral. First raise the desire to awaken; then diligently practice. Awaken to nirvana—peace, tranquility. Then cast it away and again raise up the desire to awaken. Practice some more, awaken, attain nirvana, then cast it away again.

Do the same thing over and over again, never satisfied with where you stand with your accomplishment. Putting aside both attaining and non-attaining, both having and not having, both enlightenment and delusion, just go on.

COMPASSION

A mind that is open and aware, not creating distinctions between self and others, is full of love and compassion for all beings. To become one with and live this realization transforms one's relationship with oneself, with other people, and with the whole world. To live life in this way, with love and compassion for all existence, is the embodiment of Kanzeon Bodhisattva.

I vow not to attain complete and full awakening until every sentient being has crossed over to the other shore. Now, the moment we make this bodhisattva vow, that too is great enlightenment, because at that moment we cease seeking for enlightenment. Now our whole life is about non-doing.

Out of non-doing, which means there is no self-doing, what naturally arises is sharing with others. Every situation is an opportunity to share. When we're so consumed with our own thoughts, ideas, opinions, and emotions, we simply cannot see all these numerous opportunities to share. We're constantly burning in a living hell of our own desires, attachments, emotions, and thoughts.

How do you feel when someone comes into your home to share spirituality with you? Disgusted! How do you feel when someone offers you help when you need it? Appreciative. Then it's sharing oneself, not something stinky.

When we project our own ideas on people, we draw conclusions about others and don't give them the space and freedom to change. If they do change, we don't see it. We see only our projection, not the person.

To see the situation as it is, this is called *tathagata*, suchness, another word for Buddha. When you see clearly without projecting through a filter, you are seeing Buddha and you are seeing with the eyes of a Buddha.

The opposite is also true. When we're seeing our own projections, we're neither seeing the Buddha nor seeing with the eye of the Buddha. We are seeing with the conventional eye, in a deluded or dualistic way.

W hat is it to really listen? When you listen, are you listening to hear something that will confirm or reinforce your own ideas, thoughts, and beliefs? Or are you listening in a way that will allow you to see anew?

Listening to discover something new, to find out what is true, is very different from listening merely to confirm your own beliefs. When you are listening only to confirm, then your effort really has very little value.

When you are truly open to something new, your mind is attentive, free, and unencumbered. It is not committed to something. It is very sharp, precise, alive, inquiring, and fresh.

T he question is how to listen not merely with your ears but with your whole being. When you are sitting very still, silently, with your attention not fixed on anything in particular, not making an effort to concentrate, but with the mind very quiet and attentive, then you hear everything.

You hear the sounds of the world. You hear the silence between the sounds. You hear the sounds that are close to you as well as the ones far off in the distance.

You are listening to everything. Your mind is not excluding, not keeping any sounds from entering. It is not condemning or judging. It is completely open, an all-inclusive mind, without walls or barriers around it.

There is no strain, no effort, no volition, no longer any separation between the sounds and the hearing. There is just hearing, with no gap between subject and object.

In this state of hearing something extraordinary happens. A complete transformation takes place. You are no longer experiencing the world from a fixed position as a separate individual. Now you are hearing with the ear of God, with the ears of Kanzeon Bodhisattva.

T he word *discipline* actually means to learn, to study, to discover. We watch and observe, and we learn about our own mind, who we are.

And when you learn about your own mind and who you are, you learn about everybody else, because everybody basically operates the same. So when you know yourself, you know everybody else.

When we put authority outside our self, we don't take responsibility for our own life. Wherever we are, we are constantly trying to grasp it in books, in what teachers say. We are doomed to constant frustrations and disappointments. We need to be the master of our own mind, our own life. Be the authority!

Why is that so scary? You are responsible. There is no one and nothing to rely on. You don't trust yourself enough: "I don't really know; I'm looking for someone who knows, who can be my authority."

But guess what? That person doesn't know either. So let's follow the person who pretends to know, then we never have to take responsibility for our own life!

I t's so easy to blame someone else and not take responsibility for doing our life.

Whether we realize it or not, every moment of every day we are creating our future, our destiny, our karma. What we have created is waiting right there for us in the next moment all the time.

Most of the time we are not even aware of how we are creating our own karma, so it is easy to find fault with others when karma bites us in the butt. But really there's no one to blame. We create it without being conscious of what we are doing.

We do this practice to become more conscious, to wake up and see how we are creating our karma every moment. When we see who is really responsible, something shifts. Our attitude shifts from blaming others to appreciating every moment as the teaching.

When you really empty yourself, in a certain way there's a responsibility that goes with it, because you can see so clearly that you could really devastate somebody. Everybody becomes an open book, completely naked. You see all the fear and trepidation, the anxiety and self-protection.

Maybe one reason we're so frightened of this clarity is we don't want to assume the responsibility that goes with it.

When you realize the Unborn Buddha Mind, this One Mind, you see that there is nothing to hold onto or depend on and nobody to blame. You have to own it all.

Elizabeth Kubler-Ross once said that until you realize you are capable of taking food out of the mouth of a starving baby, you'll never be enlightened. If you can't admit that you are capable of the most horrible atrocities imaginable, then how can you have true compassion? Compassion comes out of realizing I am just like that, no different, no better.

If you cannot see the Hitler within yourself, you can't save even yourself. Easy to identify yourself with Buddha, but what about the prostitute on the street, the junkie, the wino? Is it so easy? Isn't it easier to blame others, to despise others, to feel pity for others, and to keep your distance?

In Jungian terms, we have to own our shadow side. Once we stop disowning aspects of our self, we will just naturally treat everyone as Buddha.

When you really know true nature, there's abundance, there's no end. You can just keep giving it away—love, compassion, money, possessions, yourself, your energy—you don't have to hold any of it back in reserve thinking there's not going to be enough.

To give is important, but to give what a person wants is even better. Usually we have our own idea of what others should have. But sometimes it doesn't hurt to drop what we think is best and give them what they want. Try it.

W hen you're completely identified with emptiness, you are always functioning in compassion, as pure love, unconditional love. Of course, this may appear to others as loving or not, depending on the depth of their own realization.

There's the mother of compassion and the father of compassion. The mother of compassion is very giving, nurturing, supportive. The other side, the masculine side, is not afraid to use the big stick when necessary to make you wake up.

K anzeon Bodhisattva is each one of us when we are manifesting and actualizing selfless love and compassion for all beings. We are no longer identified with the small ego-centered mind but with the boundless, limitless mind that includes the entire cosmos. We are no longer seeking a secure, confined pool off to the side of the river. Instead, we are one with the continuously flowing, ever changing river of life.